DRAWING MADE FUN

MARINE MAMMALS

Robin Lee Makowski

Rourke
Publishing LLC
Vero Beach, Florida 32964

www.rourkepublishing.com

All illustrations Robin Lee Makowski.

Editor: Frank Sloan

Cover design by Nicola Stratford

Library of Congress Cataloging-in-Publication Data

Makowski, Robin Lee.
  Marine mammals / written and illustrated by Robin Lee Makowski.
     p. cm. -- (Drawing made fun)
  ISBN 1-59515-472-8 (hardcover)
  1. Marine mammals in art--Juvenile literature. 2.
Drawing--Technique--Juvenile literature. I. Title.
  NC781.M345 2006
  743.6'95--dc22
                                    2005010724

Printed in the USA

CG/CG

Rourke Publishing
1-800-394-7055
www.rourkepublishing.com
sales@rourkepublishing.com
Post Office Box 3328, Vero Beach, FL 32964

INTRODUCTION

Drawing is a skill that is fun and useful, and something everyone wants to learn how to do better.

The step-by-step instructions in this book will help you first to see what you want to draw. Then you can place the parts correctly so your finished drawing looks the way you want it to. Of course, the only way to perfect your drawing skills is to practice, practice, practice!

If the drawing doesn't look right the first time, draw it again. It can be frustrating if the finished drawing doesn't look the way you wanted it to and you don't know how to fix it.

Follow the instructions and have fun learning how to draw your favorite marine mammals!

MATERIALS

The two most common problems with drawing are not seeing how the parts of the object line up and using the wrong materials. The first problem will be solved with practice. The second problem is much easier to fix. You'll have a lot more fun and success with your drawings if you're not fighting with hard pencils, dry erasers, and thin paper.

These materials are available almost anywhere and will make your practice much easier:

Best to Use

Soft Pencils (#2B or softer)
Thick and Thin Drawing Pens
Soft White Eraser or Kneaded Eraser
Pencil Sharpener
Drawing Paper Tablet
Tracing Paper
Wax-Free Graphite Paper (helpful but not necessary)
Crayons or Colored Pencils or Colored Markers

More Difficult to Use

Typing or Computer Paper
Hard or Pink Erasers
Hard Pencils (if the pencil will mark your hand,
it's soft enough)

HOW TO START

The Shapes of Things

Everything you draw in this book will start with larger geometric shapes to get the proportions and to get everything lined up correctly. Then the details will emerge from there. One of the biggest mistakes made when drawing is starting with the outline.

By the time the outline is finished, the proportions are way off.

You'll use both standard geometric shapes and free-form shapes to start:

Laying Down the Lines

You can do your preliminary drawing—and make your mistakes—on tracing paper and then transfer it to the drawing paper. If you draw directly on the drawing paper, you can keep your drawing clean by putting a piece of scrap paper under your hand so you don't smear the pencil as you work.

When you start your drawing, use light lines so you can erase. Your preliminary shapes do not need to be perfect—they are only guidelines for your final drawing. Make sure everything lines up!

Tracing paper will take a lot of erasing. To transfer your preliminary drawing, use wax-free graphite paper between the tracing paper and drawing paper. Be sure the graphite side is down!

Draw back over the lines with a colored pencil so you don't miss transferring part of it. If you don't have graphite paper, turn over your drawing and draw with your soft pencil back over the lines. Turn it right side up; place it on the drawing paper and trace back over the lines with a colored pencil. You will have a nice, clean drawing to finish.

FINISHING

To make things easier to see and follow in the book, you can use drawing pens for the final step. Below are examples of strokes you can use if you want to finish your drawing and some tricks for making your drawings look dimensional. You can stop at Step 3 of each lesson and color your drawing, if you wish, by following the color instructions for each marine mammal. You can use crayons, colored pencils, or markers. If you use markers, color the drawing first. Then finish by drawing the lines over the color with your drawing pen. You will love the results!

You will be learning how to draw marine mammals in this book. Most of the marine mammals in this book are animals I have worked with or seen in the wild. Have fun learning how to draw marine mammals!

Practice laying down tone with your art pen by tracing around a popsicle stick to make a tone chart. 0% is white paper and 100% is solid black. For crosshatching, use thin, parallel lines that overlap as the tone gets darker:

For stippling, use the very tip of the pen to make tiny dots. Don't bang the pen hard on the paper; use a light touch to keep the dots round. Use fewer dots farther apart for lighter areas and heavier dots closer together for dark areas.
Warning: Stippling takes a long time but is worth the effort!

Now try to make the same shape look dimensional with your strokes:

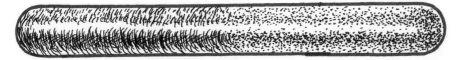

Blue Whale

Blue Whales are the largest animals that have ever lived on earth on land or sea, and they're still alive today. They can grow to well over 100 feet (30.5 meters) long and weigh about one ton per foot! A Blue Whale's heart is the size of a Volkswagen Beetle and its tongue is as big as an elephant. The most amazing thing is that the largest of all animals eats the smallest of all animals; Blue Whales filter tons of plankton from the water through a strainer, called a baleen, which hangs from the roof of its mouth. As large as they are, Blue Whales are very gentle and peaceful creatures.

1. Begin with a long, thin rectangle that tips up to the right. Use a triangle for the head (on the left) and split the triangle in half horizontally. This will be the line of the mouth. Use another triangle on the right for the peduncle, or tail stalk. Use a long, thin triangle for the pectoral fin and a half-oval for the flukes.

2. Connect the shapes to form a simple outline. Erase the areas where the shapes overlap, and any lines you don't need. Indicate the mouth and eye, noting placement. Add the small dorsal fin about two-thirds of the way back.

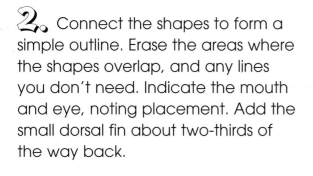

3. Draw in the ridge that runs up the top jaw, and the "splash guard" in front of the double blowholes that are the whale's nose. Draw in the large, irregular spot pattern on its back, and the rorqual grooves on the throat. These expand to form a large pouch when the whale feeds. If you want to color your Blue Whale, stop drawing now and switch to your colors.

For Color: Blue Whales are steel blue gray with darker gray spots. Sometimes a tiny animal called a diatom grows on its throat and belly. This makes it look yellow, which is why the old whalers used to call the Blue Whale "sulphur-bottom."

4. Use short strokes or stippling to indicate pattern. Make the spots darker on the back.

Bottlenose Dolphin

Among the most loved of all animals, Bottlenose Dolphins are found in all oceans of the world. They can grow to over 8 feet (2.4 meters) long, and they live in family groups called pods. Their permanent "smiles" are endearing, and their playful antics entertain millions of people in oceanariums and in the wild all over the world.

1. Begin with a large, elongated teardrop shape, as shown. Use triangles for the dorsal (back) fin, tail flukes, and pectoral fins, paying special attention to placement and size. Use an oval for the rostrum (beak).

2. Connect the shapes to form a simple outline. Erase the areas where the shapes overlap, and any lines you don't need. Indicate the line of the mouth and the eye.

3. Draw in lines indicating the pattern of tone. Notice how the lower jaw sticks out a little farther than the top. If you want to color your Bottlenose Dolphin, stop drawing now and switch to your colors.

For Color: Bottlenose Dolphins are dark gray above, light (sometimes pink) below, and gray on the sides. Their fins and flukes are the same gray as their backs.

4. To finish the drawing, start with the dark tones, then the medium tones. Add shading to the light belly, and leave the very white areas alone! Use curving strokes for the tone in thicker lines for darker and thinner for lighter. Leave a light area around the top of the lower jaw.

9

California Sea Lion

Different species of sea lions are found in most cold oceans all over the world. California Sea Lions are the species most often seen in captivity. Sea lions have an external earflap, can "walk" on all four limbs, and pull themselves through the water with their front flippers. They are members of the Pinniped family, which means "feather-footed."

1. Begin with a long, thin "potato" shape for the body and a smaller, shorter potato for the head. Connect it to the body with the two lines for the thick neck. Notice how and where the other shapes fit on and in the main shape. Use long ovals for the flippers.

2. Connect the shapes to form a simple outline. Erase the areas where the shapes overlap, and any lines you don't need.

3. Indicate the eye, earflap, nose, and mouth. Indicate the serration on the trailing edge of the front flipper and the toes on the back. If you want to color your Sea Lion, stop drawing at this point and switch to your colors.

For Color: Sea Lions can be blonde, reddish, brown, or even look black when they're wet.

Note: To indicate volume (roundness,) make sure you use curved lines around the body instead of straight up-and-down, which will flatten out the shape.

4. To finish the drawing, use crosshatching or stippling to draw in the tone. Leave the light on the back, top of the head, ear, and flippers. Draw in the back toes.

11

Elephant Seal

Elephant Seals are among the largest of the seal species. True seals push themselves through the water with their back flippers and are graceful and swift under water. On land, however, they move forward by scooting on their bellies. Bull (male) Elephant Seals have a large nose like an elephant, which they inflate to call to their mates and to challenge other bulls.

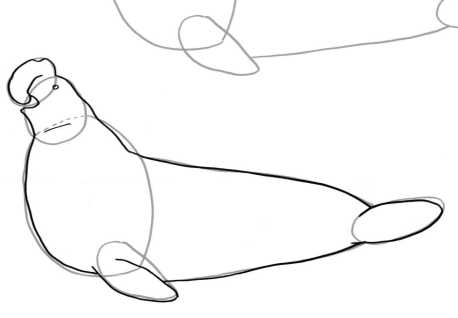

1. Begin with a stack of circles, like a snowman that tips a little to the left. A triangle shape connects the front of the body to the long oval shape at the back for the flipper. About the same size and shape oval will form the front flipper.

2. Connect the shapes to form a simple outline. Erase the areas where the shapes overlap, and any lines you don't need. Shape the great nose and draw the open mouth. Tuck the end of the nose into the mouth. Indicate the eye and notice the placement. Round out the flipper shapes and draw them up into the body.

3. Detail the face and refine the outline. Detail the folds behind the head and shoulder and around the front flipper. Separate the lobes of the back flipper and draw in the second one. Draw in the large canine tooth in the lower jaw — an important detail! If you want to color your Elephant Seal, stop drawing at this point and switch to your colors.

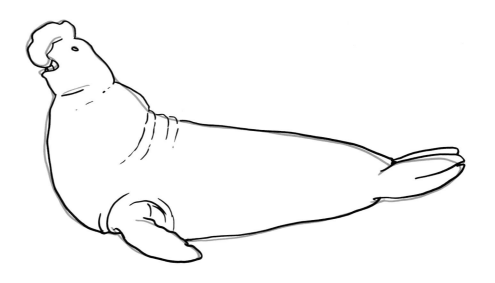

4. To finish the drawing, use short strokes to make the fur, paying attention to the direction the fur grows and to the highlight areas. Use the same stroke in the dark areas as in the light ones; just use more strokes closer together. Detail the flipper and add the toenails. Use small scribbles on the massive chest to indicate scarring from other bull Elephant Seals. They use those sharp canine teeth to fight with!

For Color: Elephant Seals are warm to reddish gray with silvery highlights.

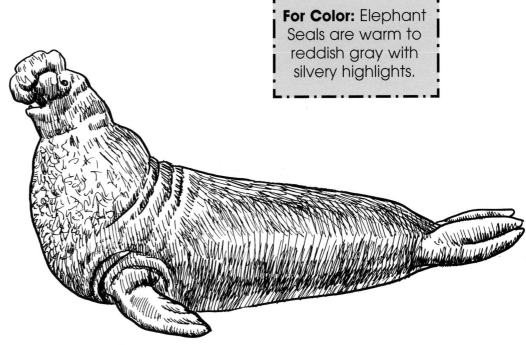

13

Harbor Porpoise

There are only six different species of True Porpoises in the world, and there are 32 different kinds of dolphins. Porpoises are shy creatures and don't normally approach boats like dolphins do. Porpoises have a triangular shaped dorsal fin and are often seen alone. Some species of porpoises, like Dall's Porpoise, travel in large herds. Harbor Porpoises are coastal and often found in harbors and estuaries in colder climates.

1. Begin with a large teardrop shape, as shown. Use triangles for the dorsal (back) fin, tail flukes, and pectoral fins, paying special attention to placement and size!

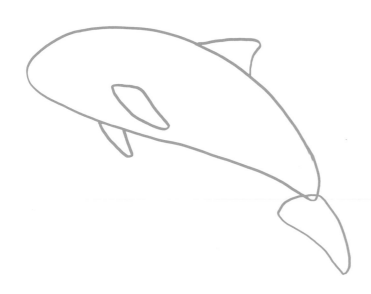

2. Connect the shapes to form a simple outline. Erase the areas where the shapes overlap, and any lines you don't need. Place the eye and line of the mouth.

3. Draw in light lines indicating the beautiful pattern on this porpoise. Notice how the lower jaw sticks out a little farther than the top. If you want to color your Harbor Porpoise, stop drawing at this point and switch to your colors.

Remember: Lining up all your shapes in the right spot will result in work you will be very happy with! Take the extra few minutes in the first steps to make sure everything is in the right place. Draw, erase, and draw again!

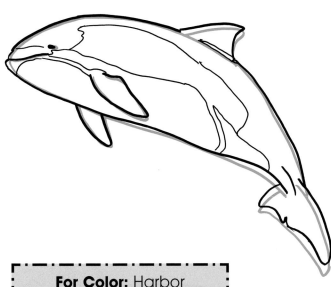

For Color: Harbor Porpoises are dark gray above and on the fins, lighter warm gray on the sides, and very light on the belly. This is called "protective coloration" because the animal is camouflaged from above and below.

4. To finish the drawing, start with the dark patterns. Then add tone to the lighter areas and leave the very white areas alone! Use curving strokes for the tone in thicker lines for darker and thinner for lighter. Leave a light area around the eye and at the top of the lower jaw.

15

Harbor Seal

Harbor Seals are among the smallest seal species. They live in cold waters along the coast. Like other true seals, Harbor Seals have a hole for their ear, front flippers that look like claws, and they can get comfortable lying across a sharp rock in the sun.

1. Begin with a large teardrop shape on its side. Use triangle shapes for the tail and front flipper and an oval for the flipper on the side. Note the placement of the circle for the head.

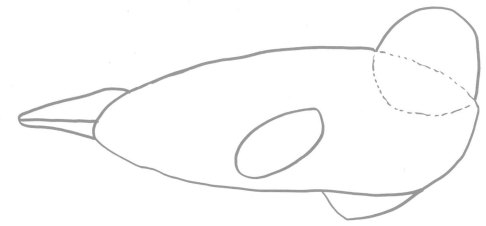

2. Connect the shapes to form a simple outline. Erase the areas where the shapes overlap, and any lines you don't need. Draw the circles for the mouth and the lemon shapes for the eyes, paying attention to placement. Shape the back flippers as shown.

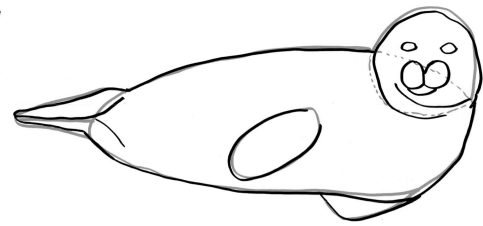

3. Detail the face and refine the outline. Draw in the finger shapes on the front flippers and the wrinkled skin around. If you want to color your Harbor Seal, stop drawing at this point and switch to your colors.

For Color: Harbor Seals are silvery light gray to dark black with dark spots.

4. To finish the drawing, use short, thin strokes to make the fur, paying attention to the direction the fur grows. Leave a nice sparkle in the eyes. Leave lighter margins around the areas of light that separate the top and bottom back flippers and around the wrinkles on the front flippers. Don't forget the long claws on the front flipper. Add some long whiskers as a finishing touch.

Fun Fact: Although the movie, Andre, depicted Andre as a sea lion, he was actually a Harbor Seal!

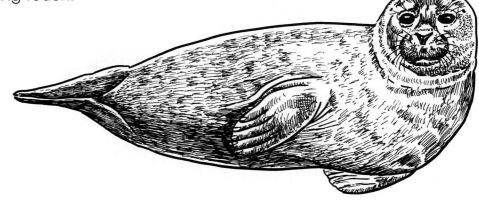

Harp Seal Pup

Harp Seals live under the ice in the frozen north. Pups are born on the ice in the winter near a hole that the mother seal keeps open so she can hunt. While she's hunting, she leaves the baby alone, and it is vulnerable to attack from polar bears. For safety, the pup's coat is snowy white to blend in with the snow, and if danger comes, it calls to its mother who hears it through the ice. After a few weeks when the pup is old enough to swim, it sheds its white coat and resembles the adult.

1. Begin with a large teardrop shape that's flatter on the bottom. Use a circle for the head and notice how it's placed within the larger shape, not to the left of it! Notice how and where the other shapes fit on and in the main shape. Use half-ovals for the front flippers and a rectangle and triangle for the back flippers.

2. Connect the shapes to form a simple outline. Erase the areas where the shapes overlap, and any lines you don't need. Add the line of the mouth and the eyes. Draw in the toes on the back flippers.

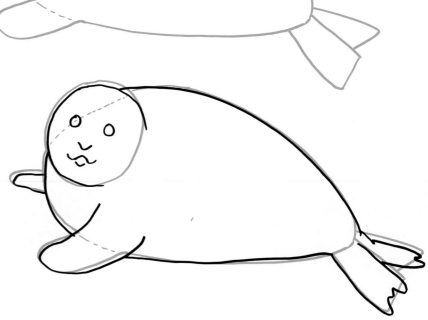

3. Detail the eyes, nose, and mouth. Use a broken line to indicate the outlines, to start to make the seal look fuzzy. Draw in the toes and the long, sharp toenails. If you want to color your Harp Seal Pup, stop drawing at this point and switch to your colors, although color will be limited to a little bit of shading.

For Color: Harp Seal Pups are snowy white with black eyes, nose, mouth, and toenails. Adult Harp Seals are smooth (not fuzzy) silvery gray with darker markings.

4. To finish the drawing, leave most of the body white. Use short strokes to indicate the fur, and stippling on the face to indicate tone. Make sure to leave a nice sparkle in the eyes. Don't forget the whiskers!

Humpback Whale

Humpback Whales are one of the best-known whale species. They can grow to a length of 45 feet (13.7 meters) and are known for their "songs." Humpbacks have long flippers that can be one-third the length of the whale! The flippers and bottom part of the tail, or flukes, have markings that are unique to each whale.

1. Begin with a free-form "S" shape for the body. Use an inverted half-circle for the flukes, and a long hot dog shape for the pectoral fin. A small shape marks the dorsal fin.

2. Connect the shapes to form a simple outline. Erase the areas where the shapes overlap, and any lines you don't need. Add the line of the mouth, which continues up over the pectoral fin as a rorqual groove. Notice how the lower jaw extends beyond the top. Place the eye. Shape the pectoral fin and serrate the leading edge, noticing how the top and bottom knobs are the largest. Shape the dorsal hump (thus the name!) and dorsal fin. Shape the flukes; the shapes vary so much that you really can't do it wrong!

3. Further refine the outline. Add the rest of the rorqual grooves (humpbacks have between 40 and 90). Detail the eye and add the knobs on the top jaw. Indicate the twin blowholes characteristic of baleen whales (toothed whales have one blowhole). Lightly draw in the areas of tone. You can't do it wrong — each is individual and like a fingerprint! If you want to color your Humpback Whale, stop drawing at this point and switch to your colors.

For Color:
Humpbacks can be reddish to dark gray to black with white markings.

4. To finish the drawing, indicate the tone with line or stippling, paying attention to the volume (roundness) of the whale. Leave the light areas light with minor shading. The pectoral fins and bottom of the flukes can be solid white to patchy like a Pinto to solid dark. Leave the white parts.

Orca

Orcas are known as the wolves of the sea. These beautiful whales are actually the largest members of the dolphin family. Orcas are born into family units called pods, with which they will live their entire lives. They communicate with a complex language of squeaks, buzzes, and whistles, and each pod has its own dialect, or "accent." Orcas are the only whale species in the ocean that have no natural enemies. They hunt anything and nothing hunts them!

1. Begin with a large, elongated teardrop shape, as shown. Use triangles for the dorsal (back) fin, tail flukes, and a "lemon" shape for the pectoral fins, paying special attention to placement and size!

2. Connect the shapes to form a simple outline. Erase the areas where the shapes overlap, and any lines you don't need. Indicate the white jaw line and draw in the tip of the other pectoral fin.

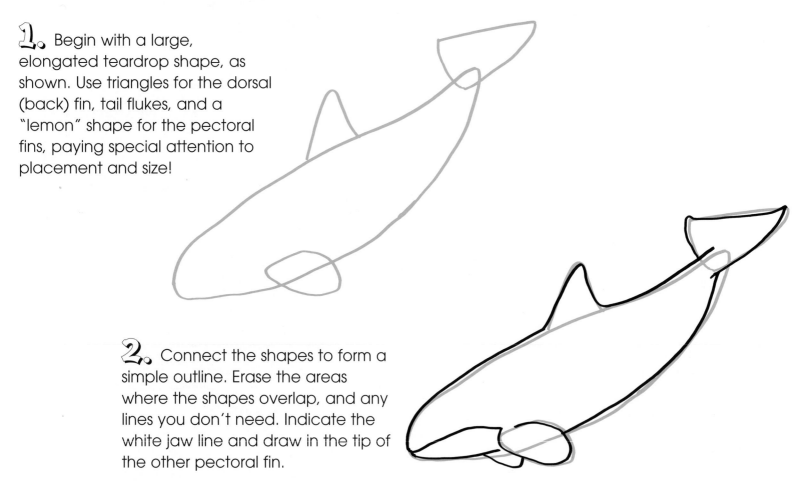

3. Draw in lines indicating the beautiful pattern on this large dolphin. Notice how the upper jaw sticks out a little farther than the bottom. Place the eye between the corner of the mouth and the false eye patch. If you want to color your Orca, stop drawing at this point and switch to your colors, although this animal has stark black and white "protective coloration."

For Color: Orcas are black and white with a dark gray saddle behind the dorsal fin. The Orca depicted is a female; to draw a male, make the dorsal fin half again as tall, straight (no hooked tip), and make the pectoral fins twice as big.

4. To finish the drawing, start with the dark parts. Add shading to the white areas, and leave the very white areas alone! Use curving strokes for the tone in thicker lines for darker and thinner for lighter. Leave a light area around the top of the lower jaw.

Tip: If you're having trouble figuring out what's wrong with your drawing, walk away from it and come back to it, or hold it up to a mirror. The mistakes will jump out at you!

Polar Bear

A Polar Bear is a marine mammal? Yes! The Polar Bear is the only large land carnivore classified as a marine mammal. Much of its life is spent at sea hunting, and nearly all its food comes from the sea. Polar Bears will hunt seals that are "logged out," or lying out on the rocks or ice out of the water, but they can also hunt and catch seals and other prey at sea.

1. Begin with a large, thick oval for the body. Use an oval for the head, paying attention to the size in relation to the body. Use an inverted triangle for the leg that looks like it's in the middle of the body. Use flat ovals for the feet and connect them to the body with lines, paying attention to the placement. Use a half rectangle for the muzzle.

2. Connect the shapes to form a simple outline. Erase the areas where the shapes overlap, and any lines you don't need. Draw the eyes, nose, and ear, paying attention to placement. Draw the legs up into the body and shape the feet. Draw in the other front foot between the front and back legs. Add the stubby tail.

3. Detail the face, toes, and "shag" the outlines, including the areas that are into the body and the tail. Notice the shape of the nose and placement of the mouth. If you want to color your Polar Bear, stop drawing at this point and switch to your colors.

4. To finish the drawing, start with the face. Pay special attention to leaving the white spaces. Stipple in tone to the lighter areas, and leave the very white areas alone! Add the long, black claws, although they're buried in the long fur.

Sea Otter

Sea Otters live in the cold waters from central California to Alaska along the coast. Sea Otters have the thickest fur of any mammal, and the top-rated fur on which all other furs are judged. The fur is so thick that the otter's skin stays dry! Sea Otters are the only marine mammals that use tools. They eat clams and other shellfish. To get them open, the otter will dive down and get a rock, then lie floating on its back with the rock on its belly, and pound the clam on the rock until the shell breaks.

1. Since some of the Sea Otter's body is under water, we're going to start with two groups of shapes. An oval on the right starts the head, mounted on a teardrop shape with a hot dog shape for the arm. On the left, free-form shapes start the crossed feet. Notice how the shape on the left is lower than on the right, and how there's about a head's width between the two groups of shapes.

2. Connect the shapes to form two simple outlines. Erase the areas where the shapes overlap, and any lines you don't need. Add the nose, eyes, and shape the mouth, paying attention to placement. Add kelp floating around the Otter and draped over it. The Otter has a rock on its belly and it's holding a clam.

3. Detail the eye, nose, and kelp, and refine the outline. Refine the legs and add the toes. If you want to color your Sea Otter, stop drawing at this point and switch to your colors.

Fun Fact: Sea Otters will wrap their little pups in kelp, a kind of seaweed that floats, to keep them at the surface while they dive for food. Giant kelp is one of the fastest growing plants on the planet, growing over 1 foot (.3 meters) per day!

For Color: Sea Otters can be reddish to brownish gray with white faces.

4. To finish the drawing, detail the eyes and nose and leave a sparkle in the eyes. Use short strokes to make the fur, paying attention to the direction the fur grows. Leave the face whiter, using really short strokes and stippling. Detail the ridges in the kelp leaves.

Sperm Whale

Sperm Whales are the largest members of the toothed whale family, which includes dolphins, porpoises, and beaked whales. Sperm whales have the largest brain of any animal; it weighs about 22 pounds (10 kilograms)! Sperm whales can dive deeper than any other whale, to 3,500 feet (1,066 meters). They hunt giant squid in water so deep that no light can penetrate. Sperm whales can communicate over hundreds of miles under water with their complex vocalizations.

1. Begin with a long rectangle that is pointed on the right and curves up. Notice the placement of the circle for the pectoral fin and the inverted triangle for the tail.

2. Connect the shapes to form a simple outline. Erase the areas where the shapes overlap, and any lines you don't need. Add the eye, line of the mouth, and lower jaw. Notice that the eye is halfway between the top and bottom of the main shape. Add a sliver of a circle for the pectoral fin on the other side. Shape the flukes.

3. Further refine the outline. Add the lump at the front of the head where the single blowhole is, and notice that it is "S" shaped. Fray the trailing edges of the flukes. Add the "stretch marks" along the whale's flanks behind the head. These furrows contract as the whale dives to depths under the pressure of the water and expand again when the whale surfaces. Add the rounded dorsal fin and ventral (belly) keel. If you want to color your Sperm Whale, stop drawing and switch to your colors. You can also color and then do Step 4 on top of the color for a great finish!

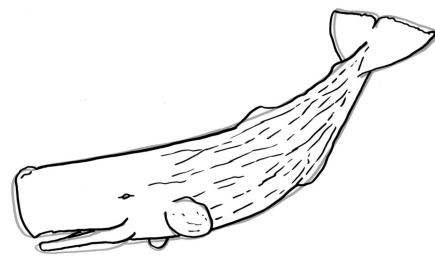

Fun Fact: You can tell what kind of whale you're looking at just by the shape of the tail flukes. All whales have a distinct tail shape unique to the species, and individuals in that species have markings on their flukes that are individual to them, like fingerprints.

For Color: Sperm Whales are dark gray, but occasionally they can be albino, or white, like Moby Dick.

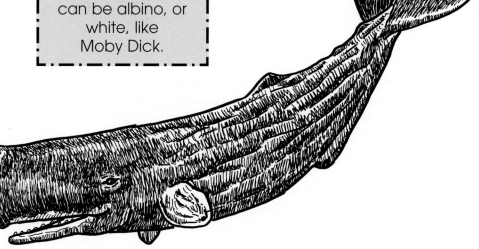

4. To finish the drawing, use short strokes or stippling for tone. Leave highlight areas on the stretch marks and around the eye, and there's a white area around the lower jaw. Add the large teeth that are only in the lower jaw.

West Indian (Florida) Manatee

Manatees are among the most endangered of all marine mammals. West Indian Manatees live around coastal Florida and the Bahamas and must stay in water that's 72° F. (22° C) or warmer, or they'll freeze to death. Manatees are gentle herbivores that graze on sea plants such as water hyacinth and turtle grasses. Their closest living relative is the elephant!

1. Begin with an elongated oval shape tilted up to the left. Use about the same size free-form circles for the head and paddle tail. Put in the shapes for the front limbs.

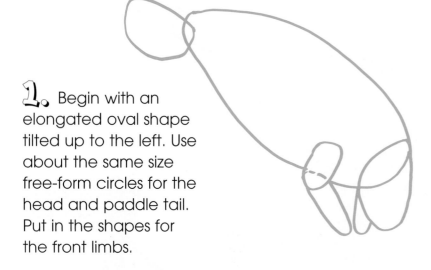

2. Connect the shapes to form a simple outline. Erase the areas where the shapes overlap, and any lines you don't need. Shape the tail and front "arms." Add the eye: notice that the placement lines up with the line that connects the head to the neck.

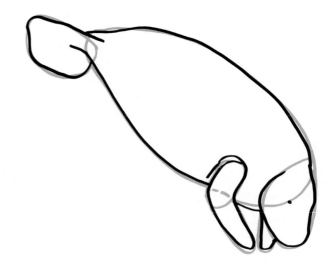

Fun Fact: Notice the shape of the toenails. Does it remind you of the toenails of any other animal? The Manatee's closest living relative is the elephant! Notice the shape of the toenails the next time you see an elephant.

3. Detail the face and refine the outline. Notice the star shape around the eye and the placement of the mouth and nose. Draw the toenail shapes and the wrinkles in the arm and around the head. If you want to color your Manatee, stop drawing at this point and switch to your colors. You can also color with your markers at this point and use the black lines in Step 4 over the markers.

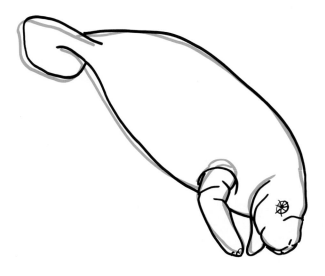

> **Remember:** Lining up all your shapes in the right spot will result in work you will be very happy with! Take the extra few minutes in the first steps to make sure everything is in the right place. Draw, erase, and draw again!

4. To finish the drawing, you can use crosshatching or stippling to indicate the tone. Use heavier strokes for the darker areas and lighter, thinner strokes for the medium tones.

> **For Color:** Manatees are medium warm gray and sometimes have greenish algae growing on their backs.

ABOUT THE ARTIST

Robin Lee Makowski is a professional artist, illustrator, and instructor. She specializes in watercolor painting and drawing and has illustrated more than thirty children's books.

"I always loved science and nature," explains the artist. "I studied everything closely and tried to draw it. I noticed the way things lined up, how close or far away things were, the way the light hit them, and how the light affected the color."

"It's so important to learn how to draw," she insists. "You have to realize that when you can draw, you're free. All you need is a pencil and paper and you can create wherever you are. Drawing is rewarding both in the process and the product."

Robin lives in Hobe Sound, Florida, with her husband, two sons, and her best friend, her mutt Casey.

Visit Robin at her website: www.rlmart.com